For my mother, with love   A.J.

Text by Antonia Jackson
Illustrations by Giuliano Ferri taken from: Anselm Grün, *Die Ostergeschichte*.
Illustrated by Giuliano Ferri © 2012 Verlag Herder GmbH, Freiburg im Breisgau
This edition copyright © 2014 Lion Hudson

Published by Lion Children's Books
an imprint of
Lion Hudson plc
Wilkinson House, Jordan Hill Road,
Oxford OX2 8DR, England
www.lionhudson.com/lionchildrens

ISBN 978 0 7459 6391 4

First edition 2014

Acknowledgments
Scripture quotations taken or adapted from the Good News Bible © 1994 published by the Bible Societies/
HarperCollins Publishers Ltd UK, Good News Bible© American Bible Society 1966, 1971, 1976, 1992.
Used with permission.

A catalogue record for this book is available from the British Library

Printed and bound in China, November 2013, LH06

The
Easter Story

The
Easter Story

Antonia Jackson ✦ *Illustrated by Giuliano Ferri*

LION
CHILDREN'S

*I*t was time for Passover. Jesus and his twelve disciples went to Jerusalem to celebrate the festival, as was the custom.

As he rode toward the city gates, people waved palm tree branches to welcome him; others spread their cloaks on the road ahead of him.

"Praise the king who comes in the name of God!" they shouted.

When Jesus saw the festival market at the Temple, he was upset.

"This should be a house of prayer," he said, "but you have made it a place to make money!" And he overturned the market stalls.

The Temple priests decided that they had to get rid of Jesus. "He is causing too much trouble," they said to each other.

Jesus and his disciples gathered for the Passover meal. He shared some bread with them. "This is my body, which is for you. Do this in memory of me."

He gave them some wine. "This cup is God's covenant, sealed with my blood. Whenever you drink it, do so in memory of me.

"I will not be with you much longer. One of you will betray me."

The disciples were shocked, but the one named Judas Iscariot had already agreed to hand Jesus over to the priests.

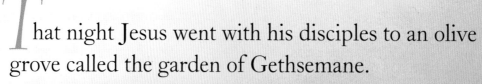

That night Jesus went with his disciples to an olive grove called the garden of Gethsemane.

He went off to pray alone and told three disciples to keep watch.

"Dear Father God," he said, "I do not want to suffer. Yet, let not what I want, but what you want be so."

When Jesus returned, the disciples had fallen asleep.

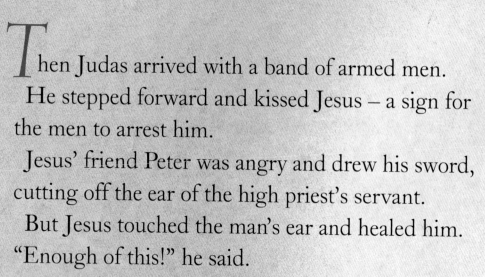

Then Judas arrived with a band of armed men.

He stepped forward and kissed Jesus – a sign for the men to arrest him.

Jesus' friend Peter was angry and drew his sword, cutting off the ear of the high priest's servant.

But Jesus touched the man's ear and healed him. "Enough of this!" he said.

The armed men took Jesus away. Peter followed at a distance.

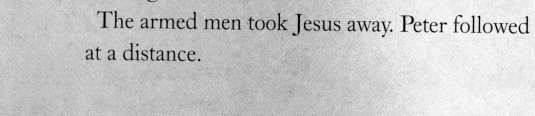

Jesus was taken to the high priest's home and put on trial.

Peter joined the servants in the courtyard there.

One woman recognized him. "This man was with Jesus!" she said.

"I don't know him," Peter replied.

Later, someone else recognized him, and then another. Both times, Peter denied knowing Jesus.

Just then, a cock crowed, and Peter remembered what Jesus had told him: "Before the cock crows tonight, you will say three times that you don't know me."

Peter went away and wept.

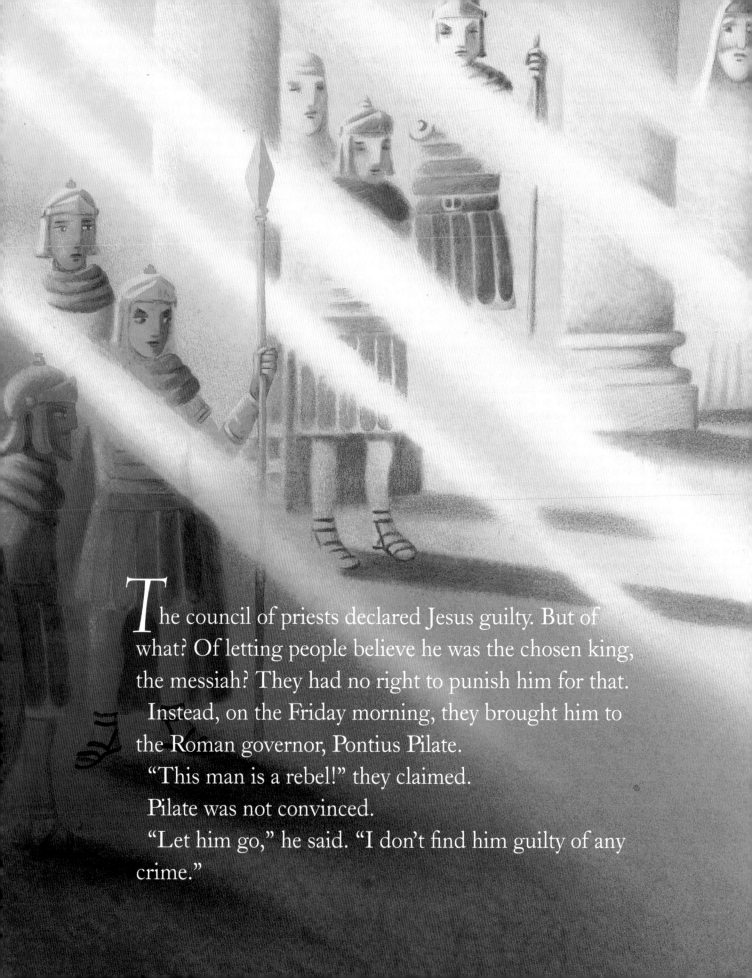

The council of priests declared Jesus guilty. But of what? Of letting people believe he was the chosen king, the messiah? They had no right to punish him for that.

Instead, on the Friday morning, they brought him to the Roman governor, Pontius Pilate.

"This man is a rebel!" they claimed.

Pilate was not convinced.

"Let him go," he said. "I don't find him guilty of any crime."

The crowds did not want Jesus to be set free.
"Crucify him!" they shouted at Pilate.
  Fearing a riot, Pilate agreed.
  The soldiers beat Jesus and mocked him.
Then they made him carry a heavy wooden cross
to the place of crucifixion.

*T*he soldiers crucified Jesus and two criminals either side of him.

Then they divided his clothes between them.

Jesus saw his mother, Mary, almost overcome with grief, and his disciple John standing close by.

"Be a son to my mother and take care of her," he said.

Not long after, he cried, "It is finished," and closed his eyes in death.

Already the sun was setting, and the sabbath day of rest was beginning.

Some of Jesus' friends took his body and placed it in a rock-cut tomb.

Early on the Sunday morning, two women went to the tomb to wrap Jesus' body properly.

The stone covering the tomb's entrance had been rolled away. An angel was there.

"Don't be afraid," the angel said. "Jesus is not here. He is risen.

"Go and tell his followers what I have told you."

Later that day, two of Jesus' followers walked to the village of Emmaus, talking about everything that had happened to Jesus.

A man joined them and explained that everything – even the crucifixion – was part of God's plan.

They asked the man to join them to eat. He said a blessing and shared some bread with them.

At last they realized he was Jesus, but suddenly he was gone.

After that, Jesus appeared among his disciples and showed them his wounds.

He shared one more meal with them, on the shore of Lake Galilee.

He spoke directly to Peter. "Do you love me?" he asked.

"You know I do," replied Peter.

Jesus asked him a second time, and a third – as many times as Peter had denied knowing him on the night of the trial.

But now Peter's love and loyalty were unshakeable.

"Take care of my flock of followers," Jesus said.

"Tell all the world the good news of God's love, which is stronger than death."